Raising Backyard Ducks

A Guide to Duck Keeping

Introduction

Thank you so much for taking the time to purchase and download my book: *Raising Backyard Ducks: A Guide to Duck Keeping.*

If you are thinking of raising ducks and are unsure where to start then you have found just the book! This book covers common terminology, duck breeds, what to expect when raising ducks, housing, feeding, to egg laying. In this book, you will find loads of helpful information to get the most out of your duck raising experience.

After reading this book, I assure you even the most inexperienced duck folks will be able to raise happy and healthy ducks with confidence! My goal is to get you excited about raising your ducks! I am excited for the opportunity to share my successes, challenges, and failures with you to help you be successful with your flock.

I started with chickens and then added ducks to the family flock. I started with five chickens about three years ago and now we have 3 female ducks, 1 drake, 30 hens, and 1 rooster. I am looking forward to spring to order new ducklings, chicks, and possibly turkeys.

Once again, thanks for downloading this book, I hope you find it to be helpful and enjoyable!

Table of Contents

Chapter 1: Terms All Potential Duck Owners Should Know

Chapter 2: Choosing a Breed(s) to Raise

Chapter 3: Creating the Proper Housing or Shelter

Chapter 4: Ducks and Water!

Chapter 5: Feeding Your Ducks

Chapter 6: Farm Fresh Duck Eggs

Chapter 7: Introducing Your Ducks to the Flock

Chapter 8: Things to Keep in Mind When Raising Your Own Ducks

Conclusion

Chapter 1: Terms All Potential Duck Owners Should Know

To ensure you get the most information and value from the chapters that lie ahead, here is a list of the most used and popular duck-related terms:

- **all flock feed:** A feed that is formulated for different types of poultry, such as ducks, chickens, pheasants, geese, and turkeys

- **bill:** The rounded beak, mouth of the duck

- **down:** The fine, soft, fluffy feathers that are on baby ducks

- **drake:** An adult male duck

- **duck:** An adult female duck

- **duckling:** A baby or young duck, may have fluffy, downy plumage

- **flock:** A name for a group of ducks

- **fount:** Watering device or a water fountain for ducks to drink from

- **gizzard:** An organ that is used to crush food with the assistance of grit or pebbles

- **hen:** Another name for an adult female duck

- **layers:** Term for matured female ducks that are kept for the production of eggs, typically at least one year old

- **laying feed:** A feed that formulated for ducks or chickens that are laying eggs

- **molt:** The process an adult goes through of losing and re-growing feathers. A hard molt is when a duck loses and regrows many feathers whereas a soft molt is when a duck loses and re-grows a few feathers.

- **poultry:** Domesticated birds including ducks, chickens, geese, and turkeys

- **preening:** The act of straightening and cleaning feathers with bill or beak

- **pullet:** A female duck that is less than a year old, not yet laying eggs

- **scratch:** A feed that is made from cracked corn and various kinds of whole grains and oats. Fed as a treat to backyard ducks and not meant to be used as a main source of food

- **sexed ducks:** Ducks that have been separated by sex

- **starter feed:** Chicken feed that is high in protein and fed to ducklings up to 8 weeks of age

- **straight-run ducks:** Ducks that have not yet been separated by sex

- **uropygial gland:** The gland near the ducks tail that secretes oil that ducks will preen onto their feathers

- **waterfowl:** Term to describe birds that swim

Chapter 2: Choosing a Breed(s) to Raise

First things first, if you live within the limits of any city, you need to take the time to check with your city council to see if having and raising ducks is allowed in your city. If you raise ducks in a city that does not allow them, you can face hefty fines. If you reside in a rural area, however, you should not have any issues with this.

The best thing to do is research and read about the pros and cons of raising your own ducks before attempting to grow a flock of your very own! I will share some common pros and cons with you later in this chapter. You can purchase ducklings, pullets, or adult ducks from a local breeder, local farm supply store, or a hatchery. I have purchased from all three. I prefer ordering from a hatchery since I am able to select the sex of the ducklings. Typically when you buy from a farm supply store they are straight run, meaning you get what you get with no guarantee of a female or male.

There are many different breeds of ducks. Some people pick their breed based on what they want to use their ducks for, such as eggs, meat, or pets. It is best to do your research before you buy any ducks to make sure the breed you choose will meet your needs. I personally bought ducks for the eggs and to diversify our flock. We have not butchered any of our ducks for meat.

The three breeds I have in my flock include Pekin, Rouen, and Khaki Campbell. The Pekin duck is the common white duck with a yellowish, orange bill most famously known for being the "Aflac" duck. This breed is primarily raised for meat, however, the hens will lay eggs too. As adults, the drake and hen will weigh between eight and ten pounds.   I currently have one drake Pekin, Sunny, and he is very docile and loves to wander around the yard. Sunny was Sunshine until we learned he was a male.

I have one Rouen hen, Midnight. This breed is a heavy breed and is not a great egg layer. I think Midnight's feathers are so pretty. She is mostly brown with some black lacing and the tips of her wing feathers have a purplish-bluish coloring to them. This breed resembles the Mallard duck in appearance especially the drakes with the white collar around their neck.

Lastly, I have two Khaki Campbell pullets, their names are Lola and Ducky. I purchased them from a hatchery as ducklings and received them in the mail.   I chose this breed since they are known for being good egg layers and also have a calm demeanor. They can lay up to six eggs per week! Our girls love to wander around the yard with the other ducks and chickens. They can be hard to catch at times but when my kids get a hold of them they do not mind being held.   This breed typically weighs between three and five pounds as adults.

Other popular backyard duck breeds include Muscovy, Cayuga, Crested, Saxony, Magpie, and Welsh Harlequin. The Muscovy duck is usually brown or black with white coloring. The males have red, fleshy growths around the base of their bill and eyes. They are typically quiet ducks and do not quack so if you have close neighbors these may be the ones for you. But on the other hand, if you are looking for a quacking duck this is probably not the breed you want.

Crested ducks have a tuft, or crest, of feathers on the top of their heads. The crest is caused by a genetic mutation. Other than the crest, Crested ducks look very similar to the Pekin as they have white feathers and yellow-orange bill and feet. Crested ducks are a medium size duck and lay anywhere from 100-130 eggs per year. This breed is mainly used for showing and kept as ornamental pets.

Cayugas have black feathers that almost appear iridescent when the light hits them and they look greenish in color. They have black bills, feet, and legs. This is a very calm breed and many people chose this breed for exhibition. One thing about this breed that I find interesting is their eggs are tinted gray in color. The hens can lay up to four eggs per week. This breed is on my wishlist for sure!

The Saxony is a great dual purpose breed as it is great for meat and eggs. Drakes have similar markings to that of the Mallard, however, their feathers are different colors. The Saxony drakes have grayish feathers on their heads and wing feathers but their bodies are brown and creamy white. The females are mostly light brown with some gray coloring on their wing feathers. This breed is inquisitive which makes them good scavengers when roaming your yard.

The Magpie lays about four eggs per week and they can vary in color ranging from white to bluish greenish. Their feathers are black and white but you might find them with blue and white coloring. The Magpie is a quiet and docile breed as well so they will make a great addition to anyone's flock.

The Welsh Harlequin is raised for show, eggs, and meat. They are great egg layers, laying up to six eggs per week. This breed is easily sexed within a few days of hatching by their bill color. The females have black, darker bills whereas the males have an orange bill. Their plumage is similar to that of a Mallard with more white coloring.

As you can see, you have many options to pick from when selecting your ducks! This is why doing your research is so important to make sure you know what you are getting. The last thing you want is to end up with a breed that does not lay eggs consistently if that is what you are looking for in your ducks.

Pros to Raising Your Own Ducks

- **Fresh eggs**: Based on my experience finding duck eggs at stores is difficult. Typically duck eggs can be purchased from local co-ops or farmers. If you are tired of paying the high prices for eggs, especially organic or cage free, having ducks lay fresh eggs right in your backyard can be a real bonus! Plus, if you have multiple hens, you will have more fresh eggs. Duck eggs are typically larger than chicken eggs and are great for baking. I think they are much tastier than store-bought eggs.

- **Meat**: Many people choose to raise ducks for their meat. Store-bought duck is pricey, so why not raise your own meat? The best thing about this is that you know exactly what your ducks are eating and how they are treated.

- **Low-Maintenance**: Ducks are very simple to take care of. Our ducks have no problem hanging out in the barn and run if we are out of town. We only need someone come check on them once a day to ensure they have enough food and water. As long as they have food, water, and shelter they are good to go!

- **Cheap Upkeep**: The expense that you will incur on a day-to-day basis when raising ducks is minimal. You can expect to spend around $25 per month on food depending on the size of your flock. The other nice thing about ducks is they will eat pretty much anything and love to explore the yard and find grubs and bugs to eat. Our ducks eat most leftovers and table scraps, along with produce and weeds from our garden. After harvesting your garden, let the ducks snoop around and eat up any leftovers. Make sure you do not allow them in the garden with seedlings as they will eat your plants, we learned that the hard way when our ducks at half our bean plants and all of our watermelon plants.

- **A Lusher Lawn and Garden**: Duck poop can be used as a natural fertilizer. If you are looking for ways to revive your garden and grass, having a few ducks around will surely do the trick.

- **Pest Control**: Ducks love to graze and forage for bugs. They love to find snails, mosquito larvae, slugs, and other insects.

- **A Fun Pet**: Ducks make a great addition to your flock. I love to watch the ducks wander around our yard and it is funny since the four of them are always together. If you raise them from the time they are young and handle them often enough, you can easily hold and pet them. They are also fun to watch waddle around and splash around in their kiddie pool.

Cons to Raising Ducks

- **Initial Costs Can Be Pricey**: Getting prepared to start your own flock from the ground up can be a bit pricey. You have to purchase hatching eggs and equipment for ducks, feed and water containers, feed, brooder, and a shelter. Ducks don't need a lot for shelter other than a place to bed down at night safe from predators. Some people will use old dog houses that are fenced in to keep the ducks safe at night.

- **Ordinances**: The rules of what pets are allowed in the backyards for those that live within city limits can vary from town to town. Make sure to check with your city regarding keeping farm animals on residential properties. The ordinances will sometimes limit the number of animals allowed or require the animals to be caged at all times.

- **Potentially Unhappy Neighbors**: If you live in a town that allows you to raise ducks, you may find that you will have unhappy neighbors. You may want to consider avoiding noisier breeds of ducks and be generous with giving out your eggs to people who have to deal with the additional noise.

- **May be messier than chickens**: Ducks can be a little messy especially with their water. They love to submerge their bills when drinking and love to take a swim and get wet any chance they get. My ducks tend to spill and splash water everywhere around their water dish. If the bedding gets too wet it may become smelly and in the Wisconsin winters gets icy.

- **Upkeep of the Shelter**: While ducks are low-maintenance, they are not zero-maintenance, but I have yet to find a pet that is. To ensure the health of your ducks, you must make it a priority to keep the shelter clean and as dry as possible. Ducks will need a steady amount of food and water.

- **Destructive Tendencies**: If you allow your ducks to roam around unsupervised, they can do some damage to your yard or garden. As I mentioned before, my ducks have nibbled on our garden plants and my flower pots. We have since learned our lesson and put up a fence around the garden to keep the ducks and chickens out.

- **Natural Predators**: Unfortunately with raising backyard ducks there are some natural predators to be aware of such as weasels, eagles, and coyotes. Be aware of possible predators in your area and prevent any problems by having a secure shelter for your ducks. Even if you take precautions, you will probably experience some loss along your journey. So far we have been very fortunate and had minimal loss with our flock over the years.

Chapter 3: Creating the Proper Housing or Shelter

First and foremost, my advice is to have a plan and a shelter set up and ready to go before buying any ducks. By being prepared, you will have a safe place for your ducks to go as soon as they arrive. Remember that ducks do not need much for shelter. They would be content with a lean-to type structure that is about three feet tall. Most ducks do not roost at night like chickens. They will make a nest on the ground or in their shelter. Since they sleep on the ground it makes them easy prey. So by having a secure shelter, it will protect them from predators at night.

My four ducks stay in the barn with our chickens during the day when we are not home and at night. Our set up is pretty simple. We converted an old horse barn into our coop. We made a run with a chain link dog kennel on one side of the barn. We have metal sheet roofing for half of the roof and then chicken wire across the other half. I have also wrapped the bottom two feet of the kennel/run and barn with cloth wire and dug it into the ground about 18-20" out from the bottom of the fence. Cloth wire is a type of fencing that looks like a small grid. You can select how big of squares you want, but I went with ½" squares to prevent any weasels from getting into our run. Burying the cloth wire will deter digging animals from getting into the shelter.

We previously built a little wood, box shelter that we kept in the barn for the ducks. I would put straw on the floor of the box to make it more comfy for them. Every time I went in the barn at night or in the morning they were never laying in their house so we ended up moving it into the run.

After I realized that the ducks were not using their shelter, we began laying straw on the barn floor. Now they just lay on the barn floor together and make little nests in it around the barn. As long as they have a place to go where they can be protected from the elements they will be happy.

When we are home, we let our ducks roam and free range the property. As I mentioned before, the four of them hang out together when they are out exploring. We also have a kiddie pool that we put out in the spring, summer, and fall. They love to splash around and preen after their bath. After they take their dip and wash up their feathers, the ducks strut around the yard showing off their fresh look. No matter where we put it in the yard they always find it. It is nice to keep the pool near the hose since the ducks make the water quite dirty, and the water needs changing almost daily.

When the evening arrives, the ducks will wander back towards the barn like the chickens. They are usually the last ones in at night especially when the weather is nice. Sometimes we have to follow behind them to get them to go in the barn. We have never let our ducks bed outside of the barn or run at night.

During the winter months, I try to avoid heat lamps or heaters of any kind since I am afraid of starting a fire. When we are expecting temps well below zero I will turn on the heat lamp and make sure there is a fresh layer of dry straw on the barn floor to help insulate the floor. My heat lamp has a metal clamp on it so I will secure it to the metal frame inside the barn. I also make sure that it is high enough that the ducks and chickens cannot knock it down. Another suggestion is to put the light on a timer switch so it turns on early in the morning and will automatically shut off midday. This winter we had a severe cold snap where the real temperature was 30 degrees below zero. During this time we did end up using a milk house heater that we secured to the rafter of the barn with a chain so it would not get knocked down. I never let the heater run when we are not home and I make several trips to the barn to ensure the heater is still running properly.

Chapter 4: Ducks and Water!

I am sure you have seen duck exhibits at the zoo or ducks in the wild floating around on a pond or lake. They love water! Not only do they love to drink lots of water, but they also love to play in water. When ducks drink water they submerge their bill when drinking. Once you get your ducks, you will notice that they have small holes or nostrils on the top of their bill. They dip their bills to flush water through these holes which helps them swallow their food.

In our barn, we use a heated dog water bowl during the cold winter months. This way the water does not freeze. A negative to using the dog dish is the ducks tend to walk in it which causes it to get dirty. This year I bought a heated water fount base that keeps the water from freezing as well. The water fount is a metal water can that holds three gallons of water compared to the one-gallon dog dish, which makes hauling water to the barn less frequent. You can buy a water fount and heated water base at your local farm supply store or online for around $60-$70 for both.

Another option is to purchase a plastic water fount which can come in various sizes and are a little cheaper than the metal ones. One thing to remember is to make sure you do not buy the founts with the nipples on them. These are intended for chickens so they can peck at them to get the water. Also remember that ducks like to submerge their bills in water so having a fount with a ring, or dish around the bottom is best.

One thing I learned about raising ducks that makes them different from chickens is they drink a lot, and I mean a lot of water! I would say on average our ducks drink easily almost half a gallon of water per duck per day. Their water intake will vary depending on their age and the season.

Water also plays a large role in allowing the ducks to keep clean.

The ducks will preen after they swim or access to dip their heads under water. When you have ducks of your own, you will see them grooming and preening themselves with their head. The ducks will rub their head by their tail feathers where their body excretes oil from the uropygial gland. They will use their head and bill to spread this oil on other parts of their body. When the ducks submerge in water you can actually see the water bead up on their feathers and roll off. The crazy part is when I pet our ducks I do not feel any oil and their feathers are very soft.

If you choose to get ducklings, keep in mind that they do not produce oil like an adult duck. This oil helps them stay dry and repel water allowing them to swim better. In the wild or if you have a hen that has hatched her ducklings, the mother will rub her oil on the ducklings. Baby ducklings should not be unsupervised when playing in water. Even their water dish should be shallow in case they were to fall in and drown or get chilled.

I have purchased ducklings at various life stages. We have gotten them just hatched, so less than 24 hours old, and purchased them up to 4 weeks old. I enjoyed getting them right after hatch because they are so tiny, fluffy, and cute! We received our shipment around the first of April and with Wisconsin's unpredictable weather I did not want them in our unheated barn or garage, so we converted a storage tote into their temporary house which ended up in the dining room. This way I could monitor their behavior and watch to know if they were too cold, too hot, or just right.

After they were a couple days old, we put them into the bathtub with about an inch of lukewarm water. We would only let them waddle around for a little bit, so they did not get cold. Once they were finished we would quickly dry them off with a towel and put them back in their house under the heat lamp. As they got bigger we would put more water into the bathtub each time to allow them to swim around. They are so adorable swimming around the tub! Some people will let them swim around in a washtub or utility sink too. Either way, it allows for easy clean up after they are done.

A good rule of thumb would be to watch your ducklings drinking water and splashing around to see if the water repels on their downy feathers. Once the water starts to repel, it is safe to allow them to swim around unattended and to provide a deeper water dish. Typically ducklings will start producing their own oil around ten weeks.

Chapter 5: Feeding Your Ducks

I must admit this is one lesson I learned the hard way with raising day-old hatched ducklings. It is worth the extra money to buy a high-quality feed.

Our first two ducklings were about 4 weeks old when we bought them from a local farmer. We put the ducklings in with chicks that were about the same age and they all ate chick starter with no issue. This made it very simple since I only needed one pen for all of the babies and did not have to worry about keeping the ducklings separate with different feed.

When we purchased our first day-old ducklings, Lola and Ducky, I started them out on chick starter as I had previously done with my Midnight and Sunny. The chick starter has a little more protein along with proper nutrients and vitamins for your growing baby. After about a week or two Lola had quite noticeable hip bones. She also walked a little slower and did not behave the same as Ducky during water play time.

I had done a lot of reading prior to getting ducks, and I remembered reading about a condition that baby ducks can get called "splayed leg." The most common trait is the legs face outward and can result in the duckling not being able to walk properly if the condition is not treated. After further research, I learned that splay leg can happen if the duckling does not have enough niacin in its diet or if it is housed on a smooth service. I had lined the storage tote with a couple layers of paper towel and covered the paper towel with wood shavings, so I knew it was not too smooth or slippery for them. I felt terrible for Lola because with each day she walked around less. It almost seemed as if she was stepping on her own feet and tripping herself.

The first thing I tried was to find foods I had around the house that naturally contain niacin. I tried to mash up ripe bananas but neither of them was a fan of those. Another option was eggs so I scrambled up eggs and fed them to Lola and Ducky once they cooled down. They both gobbled up the eggs each time. I decided to try giving them one scrambled egg twice a day for a day or two to see what would happen. Unfortunately, the eggs did not do the trick.

After about a week of her having noticeably deformed legs and difficulty walking, I decided to call the local farmer that I had previously purchased ducklings from. I shared what was happening with Lola and she said she had not experienced this before. She said to try some electrolyte powder with additional vitamins that she had used with her lame ducklings and chicks to perk them up along with changing them from a chick starter feed to a more expensive all flock feed. That evening I went to her house and picked up the powder and she gave me some all flock feed to try. From then on, I mixed about a tablespoon of the powder into their water twice a day. The next morning I also went to the local feed store to buy the all flock feed which was about $20 for a 50 lb bag, whereas the chick start is around $12 for a 50 lb bag.

After a couple of days of using all flock feed and using the electrolytes in the water, Lola's legs did not seem to improve so I turned to the internet to do some additional research about how to increase niacin in their diets. I found a couple of different sources and bloggers who actually bought niacin capsules, opened the capsules, and mixed the powder with the duck water. I decided to give this a try since I wanted to avoid bringing her to the vet.

I bought niacin capsules from the dollar store, opened the capsule and put about half of the powder in their quart size water dish at a time. I did this once a day and magically after about three to four days, Lola seemed to be walking better. By this time, it was now the end of April and some days were sunny and mild so I put them in the yard in an enclosed pen where they could eat grass and bugs. After a couple of weeks Lola's legs no longer looked turned out, and she was walking normal and able to get in and out of the pool with Ducky.

I was so thankful that she was back to normal since it killed me to see her stumbling around. By the time they were both feathered out, which was about 6-8 weeks old, they were beginning to wander around the yard with the other ducks eating grass and bugs along with their feed. Now Lola is about 10 months old and you would never know she had leg problems as a duckling.

From this experience, I learned to give ducklings all flock feed until they are about 20 weeks old and then I switched them to layer feed with our other ducks and chickens. I also think it benefits the ducks greatly to eat grass, bugs, and whatever else in nature they can find to supplement their diet. You can continue to feed adult ducks all flock feed if you would prefer. I chose to give my ducks layer feed since our ducks reside in the barn with our chickens and use the same feeders and water founts. We have not had any issues, and everyone in the flock is thriving and doing great!

Chapter 6: Farm Fresh Duck Eggs

The most exciting thing about owning ducks, or other poultry, is finding the first egg! Ducks will typically begin to lay eggs anytime between 20-30 weeks of age. From my experience, it is usually closer to 25 weeks, and I have always gotten my ducklings in the spring.

Your duck's breed will determine their egg production. Some duck breeds are better known for laying eggs. For example, Lola and Ducky are Khaki Campbells and will lay about 300 eggs per year. Both of our Khaki Campbells lay almost every day and we easily receive 5 eggs per week per female. Midnight, our Rouen female, lays every other day, definitely not as frequently as the other girls.

Duck eggs look different from chicken eggs. The first differences are the color and feel of the shells. The egg shells are a creamish color and are smoother than chicken eggs. Duck eggs can range in colors from white, green, or gray. Another contract is that they are larger than chicken eggs.

I personally think duck eggs have a slightly richer flavor. I had never eaten a fried duck egg until we had our own duck eggs. And my kids love to eat fried duck eggs too! When you crack open a duck egg you may notice that the shell is a little thicker than a chicken egg. The egg will definitely fill your frying pan too! The yolks are larger and there is more egg white. Many people use duck eggs for baking since they keep baked goods moist.

Another thing to keep in mind is ducks do not typically use nesting boxes. Midnight used to lay eggs in the nesting box with my chickens when we had a ramp walkway to the nesting area. Now that we rearranged the barn and have the nesting boxes mounted to the barn wall, my ducks lay on the floor of the barn. Occasionally we will find an egg in the run too.

Fun Facts About Duck Eggs

I am going to share some fun facts about duck eggs that I learned once we started raising ducks. As I mentioned earlier, duck eggs are great for baking since they keep baked goods moist and fluffier. I like to use duck eggs when I make egg bakes since I get a lot more egg bake with a dozen duck eggs compared to chicken eggs.

Another unique characteristic of duck eggs is some people with egg allergies are able to eat duck eggs without a reaction. I am no physician, so please ask a medical professional prior to trying this! I have spoken with a couple of people who did not have any reactions when they ate duck eggs.

Duck eggs are believed to last longer than chicken eggs due to their thicker shell. The thicker shell also makes them good eggs to decorate for Easter. My rule of thumb is I only leave non-washed eggs on the counter for no longer than a day. I always immediately refrigerate any washed and dried eggs. Also in the winter months, when I bring cold eggs into the house they develop moisture on them. I try to wash them right away and put them in the refrigerator after I dry them with a clean towel.

Some people believe that duck eggs are healthier than chicken eggs because they have higher amounts of omega-3 fatty acids and more protein and vitamins. I believe the diet of the duck is going to impact the nutritional value of the eggs. If ducks are able to roam your yard and eat grass, insects, worms, etc. they will have richer, healthier eggs than those that are only eating all flock or layer feed.

Chapter 7: Introducing Your Ducks to the Flock

You will quickly realize that your ducklings grow rapidly. The next step may be integrating your new ducks with the rest of the flock. This may be a stressful time, and I have been very fortunate to not have experienced issues when introducing our ducks.

When you introduce your new ducks to the existing flock, you will witness the "pecking order" being established. My first time introducing ducks, I noticed my older hens giving an occasional peck when the new ducks approached the feeder. The older girls want to be sure the new ducks know they are at the bottom of the order.

Last spring I introduced our two new ducklings to our existing flock which included chickens, a drake, and a hen. One thing that I did not expect to happen was the drake's nonstop attempts to mate with my little ducklings. When I introduced the ducklings to the barn, they were completely feathered out and almost ten weeks old. Within a few days, one of the little ducks had missing feathers on the back of her neck. I had seen Sunny do his thing with Midnight, but she has never had missing feathers on the back of her neck.

I quickly had to establish a new plan. We ended up putting the ducklings in the back portion of the covered run and put up a barrier so the other ducks and chickens could not get to the little ducks. This way everyone could see each other through the fencing to get to know each other better. We kept Lola and Ducky separate for a couple of weeks.

Our second attempt to introduce them went much smoother. Also by this time, the weather was warmer, and we would let the flock run around the yard. When Sunny would get too close, Lola and

Ducky would run away from him. Luckily for them, they were faster than him most of the time!

Looking back we really did not have any issues with our chickens when introducing the ducks. I think that my older chickens pick on the new chickens more than the ducks. One challenge of having all of the ducks together with the chickens is the feed situation. I like to feed my hens a layer feed but I did switch everyone to an all flock feed until Lola and Ducky began laying eggs. At that time, I ended up switching everyone to a layer feed. I like to use one type of food since everyone shares the feeder, and it is nearly impossible to know who is eating what food. I also like to give them treats that include cracked corn, oats, scratch grain, and fresh produce once in a while.

Chapter 8: Things to Keep in Mind When Raising Your Own Ducks

The best guidance I can give you is to read, read, and read some more about the different breeds and raising ducks. When I initially researched ducks, I learned that you should always start with at least two or three at a time. This way they always have a partner especially if something were to happen to one of them.

Companionship

The first time I purchased ducklings, I decided to start out with two. We converted an old metal stand up filing cabinet shelf into a brooder pen. When the cabinet was laid flat it was almost four feet wide by five feet long and about two feet deep. Since it was late spring, the weather was mild, and we decided to put the brooder pen in the barn. This way the other chickens could see the ducks through the top netting but they would be kept safe.

As I mentioned, it was springtime, so we received a lot of rain. Our barn is an old horse barn converted to a chicken coop with a dirt floor. When we get a lot of rain, the barn will get quite wet especially towards the back since the barn is in a lower spot in the backyard. I knew we had received significant amounts of rain the night before but did not think much about it since I knew the ducklings were in the two-foot deep brooder/file cabinet.

As I approached the barn, I could hear one of the fluffy ducklings making noise, a lot of noise. When I entered the soaking wet barn and approached the brooder, I saw standing water, an inch or two deep. In the standing water was one of my ducklings who had drowned and the other duckling, Midnight, was standing on top of her dead companion. I could not believe that one of my ducklings had drowned or died from being so wet and cold.

Now I was left with only Midnight and she was not happy. She would not stop making noise. I remembered reading about how ducks are very much companion animals and how they like to be with others. This is when I contacted a local poultry farm and bought two more ducks. One was named Shadow, a Rouen, and the other was named Sunshine a.k.a. Sunny, a Pekin. As soon as we put the new ducklings in with Midnight, she was quiet. It was so crazy to see and made my heart melt. I felt so terrible for what had happened in the barn and losing that little duckling.

Loss to Predators

We had three ducks in our flock for several months. During the spring, summer, and fall months we allow our flock to roam the yard. During the summer months, my husband and children are home during the day, so there is a lot of activity outside at our house. One day I came home from work and my husband said there were only two ducks walking around the yard. He said he had not heard or seen anything unusual throughout the day, but one of the ducks was missing.

During the hot summer months, the ducks like to bed down in the weeds along the side of our yard. We think that an animal must have gotten our one duck since we have seen fox, coyotes, and stray cats in the area. We did not find any feathers, so maybe she wandered off and either could not find her way home or was prey to some predator.

Flying Away

Some people have had issues with ducks flying over fences and flying away. I have not seen our ducks fly much. They do like to flap their wings a lot, especially when they swim. I have never seen them get more than a few inches off the ground, and it was for a very short distance. Some people clip their duck's wing feathers, but I have never personally done this.

Ducks Can Drown

When ducklings have their downy fluff and are recently hatched they may not be able to swim well or regulate their body temperature. The best thing to do is observe and monitor any water play until the duck is feathered out. This way the feathers will have oil on them to repel water. A duckling's downy fluff does not contain oil which will cause them to be very wet and chilled. Also, it is possible that the ducklings could tire easily which is why it is best to supervise them in the water.

Conclusion

I want to congratulate you for making it to the end of *Raising Backyard Ducks*. Thanks again for taking the time to download and read this book!

You should now have a better understanding of what it takes to start your very own flock of ducks. While there are many intricate steps to choosing the right breeds, following this easy step-by-step guide will have you raise strong, productive ducks that will be laying eggs before you know it!

If you ever have questions or other issues when it comes to the proper raising of your birds, flip open this book. You will more than likely find the answer at your fingertips.

If you enjoyed this book, please take the time to leave me a review on Amazon. I appreciate your honest feedback which helps me write high-quality books. Are you interested in learning about raising backyard chickens? If so, you should check out my book *Raising Backyard Chickens: A Guide to Chicken Keeping From Incubating Eggs, Caring for Chicks and Feeding Chickens to Egg Laying Hens*.

Printed in Great Britain
by Amazon